LET'S PRAY

by Lillian Ruxton
with additional material
by Riccardo Barnes

Cover Design and Graphics by Ron Branagan

Ruxton, Lillian
    Let's pray.
    I. Title
    242'.82

    ISBN 0-948834-06-4

CONTENTS

PAGE

Introduction	4
Beginnings, Endings and Graces	8
Special Occasions	14
Seasons	21
Praise	25
Problems and Challenges	28
Feelings	39
At Camp	44

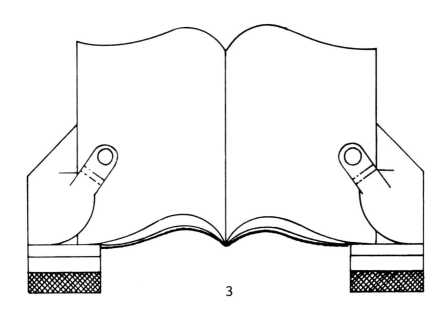

INTRODUCTION

Many parents pray with their children from a very early age, although others find this difficult. An early introduction to the concept of prayer will help build this valuable "habit", but it is not until the child is a little older that he or she will begin to understand quite what is going on. A birthday can be a good place to start. The child will already have enjoyed the delights of Christmas, and, hopefully, have learnt from his parents the true significance of the Festival. Carols like 'Away in a Manger' will be among his first songs. Next in importance to him in the following year will be his birthday. Again, the chief joy will be the PRESENTS. This is a good starting point for regular prayers. After thanking parents, aunts, uncles, friends for gifts, this is a natural opportunity for thinking of the God-given blessings of health, sight, hearing, friends, etc. - the list can be as long as you can make it. You will find appropriate 'Thank You' prayers for each succeeding birthday till the age of eight, when most children leave their first school.

This is a very big step forward into the unknown world of new teachers and real 'work' after three years of familiar and enjoyable activities in the 'Infants'. The child who by this time has a real Friend and Helper is well equipped to face new challenges.

From this period, school and group activities outside the home will take up a great deal of his time. Joining a youth organisation will satisfy the need to belong to a 'Gang' of some

sort. The many aspects of such organisations can play their part in producing the kind of well-rounded Christian citizens we hope our children will become.

I hope that this little book will be of some help to the Leaders of youth organisations, and perhaps to parents too. Both bear truly a great responsibility and their influence is particularly important today. Sincerity of feeling and the example of personal faith expressed in prayers 'from the heart' will always make a greater impact than those read from a book. That is not to say that the great and beautiful Christian prayers should never be quoted. On the contrary, the fact that they have lasted through centuries gives them the right still to be remembered for their beauty.

Prayer involves listening as well as talking to God. Listening for his guidance in solving everyday problems, and sharing with Him our inmost thoughts and feelings.

Traditionally young children are taught to pray with their eyes closed and hands together. It is valuable to encourage children to approach prayer as a special time, quietly and calmly. It is also important not to ascribe any 'magic' to this, however, and to help them feel (as they grow older) that they can pray any time, any place. As they wake in the morning, or travel on the bus, or wait for an exam to start, they can share their thoughts, hopes and fears with God, who is always with them.

Encourage the children to learn the value of silence, and being still. If the prayers follow an activity of great exertion, it is a good idea to get them to quieten down, take a few deep breaths to slow the pulse, and stand or sit quietly for a moment to gather their thoughts.

Silence at the end of prayers is also valuable, as it provides space for the children's own thoughts and prayers.

This book is intended to help adults to pray with young children. There is no doubt that the best prayers come from the hearts and minds of the people praying them, and you will therefore find a few blank pages at the end of this book for you to add prayers of your own.

Why not take this further, and put together a Prayer Scrapbook with your young people. It could include prayers you write, prayers they write, and favourite prayers collected from other sources.

It will be clear that this book is written with the Christian tradition in mind. We appreciate that many adults will be working with young people of other faiths, a mixture of faiths, or no faith at all. These are outside the scope of this book, but may be dealt with in future publications.

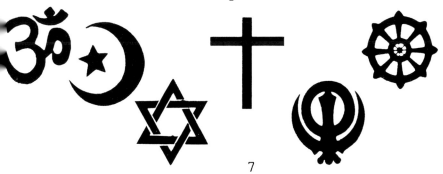

BEGINNINGS, ENDINGS AND GRACES

It is good to begin and end each day with a prayer. The first part of this chapter contains some suggested prayers for these moments, although they may also be used, perhaps with a little modification, at the beginning or end of an evening meeting, session, or camp.

The second part of this chapter contains some Graces to be said before meals. It can be helpful to vary from the usual 'For what we are about to receive.....' from time to time. It is also a good idea to ask one of the youngsters to say Grace, and indeed to involve them all as much as possible in the other prayers in this book.

AT THE START OF THE DAY

The sun has risen Father on this new day,
Show me how to follow your Son's way.
In my actions and words
and my thoughts and play
Let your will rule them all
Till the sun goes down, on this your day.

Amen

Once more our eyes are open
To face another day
We thank You for refreshing sleep
Now by our side please stay

What'er this day may bring
Of sorrow, joy or fear
We know You're there to help us
We feel Your Presence near

Amen

O Lord, our Father in Heaven, we thank You for
this new day, and all the new experiences it
will bring. For the fun we'll share with our
friends and family. May we feel secure in
Your Presence wherever we are and whatever we
are doing. We know You love us as Your
children. In return may we do our best to be
worthy of Your love in all our thoughts and
deeds.

Amen

All through the day
I humbly pray
Be Thou my Guard and Guide

My sins forgive
And let me live
Blest Jesus by Thy side

Amen   (Joseph Barnby)

STARTING A NEW SESSION

O, God our Father, we thank You for this
chance of meting together once again at the
start of a new term/year/session.

We ask Your blessing on our Group. May Your
wisdom guide our Leaders and Your Spirit be
present in all our activities. Help us to
encourage one another. To think always of the
good of the Group - not our own prestige.
Keep us true to our promises. Forgive us when
we fall short of the best that is in us. "If
we forget Thee, do not Thou forget us". Help
us to live always as in Thy Presence. Let
nothing be hid from Thy Loving eyes. Through
Jesus, our Saviour, Who taught us to pray "Our
Father.....

AT THE END OF THE DAY

Dear Lord, I'd like to trade
A range of problems for your solutions
And weaknesses which need your strength.

Perhaps my stresses for your calm
And failures seeking forgiveness
I'd like Salvation, a package deal.

I only have myself to give
But then that's all you ask
Dear Lord, I'd like to trade

Amen

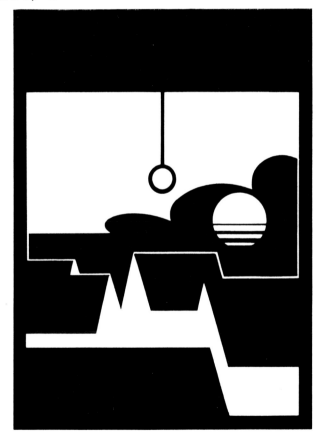

As I sleep Father
Let this prayer
Travel round the world
Bringing help to the suffering
And comfort to the bereaved

Amen

The day sped by
Where did it go?
Did I learn from you
Or seek to know?

A helping hand
Or friendly smile
Did I provide
For just a while?

A word of witness
Or loving glance
Did I give you
An even chance?

For my failures
Now in the past
I ask your forgiveness
Both first and last

Amen

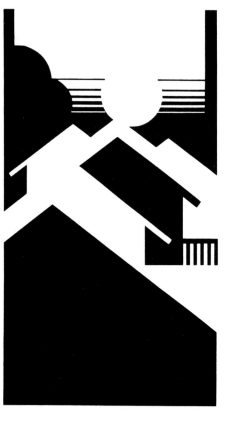

The fun and the laughs are all over. May Your
Holy Spirit go with us.   We're ready for
supper and sleep.   And all through the night
safely keep.

Amen

12

GRACES

Bless this earth, Lord, and the sea
Bless this food, Lord, prepared for me
Bless this soul, Lord, given to thee

Amen

For this food before us Father
We thank you

For our fellowship together Father
We thank you

For Christ's presence amongst us Father
We thank you

Amen

Bless this food which now we take
And make us good for Jesus' sake

Amen

Some ha'e meat, and canna eat
And some wad eat that want it
But we ha'e meat, and we can eat
And sae the Lord be thankit.

Amen   (Robert Burns)

There are a number of days in the calendar which provide a ready-made theme for a prayer, and we have selected some of these for this chapter. At the end of the book you will find some blank pages for you to add your own prayers - perhaps for other special occasions you wish to mark in this way, or perhaps for other prayers on a variety of subjects.

NEW YEAR

One year out, another in
May your peace replace the din
Of noise and confusion, war and strife
You mean for us a better life
A heart to flourish and a soul to love
In the joy of Christ and the Spirit's Dove

Amen

EASTER

The first Spring days remind us
That Eastertime is near
And soon there'll be Good Friday
With sadness hard to bear

For on that day our Saviour
By cruel men betrayed
Paid the ransom for our sins
What love was there displayed!

But three days on from that sad day
God's Son came back alive
And now, dear Lord, You're with us still
To You our hearts we give

Amen

We were sad when You died, Lord Jesus,
our Friend
But today we remember it wasn't the end
A miracle happened on that Easter Day
You came back - and promised forever to stay.

Though we can't see You, we know You are there
Please keep us, your Children, in Your loving
care.
Amen

Jesus, You're alive today
We cannot see You, but we know
We can talk and you will listen
You will help your child to grow

Grow in love and grow in wisdom
Thinking less of selfish needs
Caring more for friends and neighbours
Following where our Saviour leads

Amen

CHRISTMAS

Christmas is the very best
Season of the year,
Thank You, God for presents
And fun which we all share

Christmas only started
The day that You were born.
The shepherds brought You presents
That far-off winter's morn.

So now we give <u>our</u> presents
To friends and family dear
Help us to go on giving
Throughout the coming year.

Amen

May the 'Glow' of Christmas
Last throughout the year
To warm our hearts with kindness
And fill our days with cheer.

Amen

Bless this Christmas Father
Especially for those who are alone
And those who are sick
For those who do not receive presents
Let the free gift of your Son
Enter their lives

Amen

HARVEST

Dear Lord
May this your Harvest
By your love
Be blest

Amen

ST. PATRICK'S DAY

Lord we remember today
Your servant Patrick
To be sure he followed the way
Patrick followed the way
With Christ on his left
And Christ on his right
No matter whether day nor night
Remember us Father, we would
To be sure, like Patrick, follow the way

Amen

ST. GEORGE'S DAY

St. George and England
Heart and Home
Though elsewhere
I might roam

A special place
I keep within me
Reserved for
Divinity

This I honour
Wherever I roam
From George and England
Heart and Home

Amen

ST. DAVID'S DAY

Mountain and sea
Hill and dale
Saw David's face
Both hearty and hale

A heart of gold
A legend of old
David trusty and true
Could I be too?

Amen

ST. ANDREW'S DAY

Lord, Andrew knew you;
Let us know you.

Lord, Andrew shared his life with you;
Let us share our lives with you.

Lord, Andrew loved you;
Let us also love you.

Amen

GUY FAWKES

Whizz, flash, bang and splutter
How our hearts jump and flutter
Lights and colour, whoops and mutter
In rowdy din we can but stutter
Thank you Lord

Amen

BIRTHDAYS

Four-year old

Thank you, God for birthdays
Thank you, God for friends
Thank you for the cakes and cards
And presents Granny sends

Amen

Five-year old

Father, God, bless me
Now I am five
It makes me so happy
To know You're alive

Amen

Six-year old

Today, God I'm six
I've had lots of fun
With friends at my party
They came ev'ry one!

And now I'll say 'Thank you'
Dear Father in Heaven
I know You'll stay with me
Until I am seven

Amen

Seven-year old

I'm seven years old today
I'll soon get up to eight!
Then please go with me Father
Past the INFANT'S GATE

When everything is strange and new
And schoolday hours so slow
New teachers, too, and lots of work
You'll help me, God, I know!

Amen

The changing of the seasons reminds us of the careful orderliness of the world, and of the greatness and goodness of God. These prayers pick up the theme of each season, and help the children to think about the Creator who established them - and everything else.

SPRING

Thank You for the new green shoots in the fields
For the fresh, soft sweetness of the air.
For the scent the lilac blossom yields
And the song of the lark beyond compare!

Amen

The seeds have started growing
The winter cold has gone
We thank You, God our Father
For wind and rain and sun

Amen

Thank You, God, for the wind that dries and warms the earth, so that seeds may grow; giving us food to eat and flowers to see and smell.

Thank you too, for fun outdoors on windy days.

Amen

How pretty to watch are the ducklings
As after their mother they swim!
Take care of them, please, loving Father
Their eyesight is still rather dim!

Amen

SUMMER

Thank You God, for longer days
Now summertime is here
For outdoor games and holidays
In places far and near

Be with us at the seaside
Be with us as we play
Be with us as we climb the hills
Or sail across the bay

Amen

For the glorious land we live in,
For the hills and streams, cornfields and
meadows;
For the men and women who have spent their
lives serving their country

(Response)   We thank you, Lord.

Amen

AUTUMN

Now we're back from holidays
Time to work we say
New classes, friends and teachers
Stay with us, Lord, we pray

We need Your help at all times
Specially when we find
It's hard to love as you do
When others are unkind

Amen

23

Thank You, Lord for autumn
And blust'ring winds from the west
For falling leaves as they flutter down
All golden and scarlet and russet brown
As Nature prepares for her rest

Amen

WINTER

Thank You, God, for snowballs
And for berries bright
Thank You for the beauty
Of gardens smooth and white

The snow is like a blanket
Keeping seedlings warm
Thank You for the flowers
That later on will form

Amen

The cold wind and the freezing air
Have stripped the trees of their leaves
And yet we thank You, Father
For the beauty Winter gives.

We see trees black against the sky
Their whole shape now defined
The pattern of their limbs and twigs
Were by Your hand designed

Amen

There is so much to be thankful for, and for all of it we have to thank God. In this chapter we have selected a small range of subjects for prayers of praise. This is an ideal form of prayer for the children to compose for themselves. Encourage them to do so, and retain the best for future use. The few we present here are to get you started.

FOR FRIENDSHIP

Lord Jesus, I thank You for my friends. It's good to know they like being with me and I with them. Help me always to choose the right friends and, in turn, may I be loyal and true to them.

Amen

FOR UNDERSTANDING

Heavenly Father, open our eyes to <u>see</u> what is beautiful, our minds to <u>know</u> what is true, our hearts to <u>love</u> what is good. Through Jesus Christ our Lord.

Amen

FOR SKILLS

Steady hand and certain sight
Speed and swiftness, gentle might
These gifts you gave us - teach us too
To use them wisely - and for you.

Amen

FOR CREATIVITY

Lord we praise you for Music and Song
These gifts you granted to help us along
Lord we thank you for Art and Dance
For each of us you provide a chance
Lord we worship you for Drama and Speech
And being able to learn and to teach
Lord we exalt you for Writing and Verse
Though our attempts could not be worse
Lord we love you for Life and Light
For we are all precious in your sight

Amen

FOR NATURE

The large and the short
And the grunt and the snort
The fox and the owl
And the midnight howl
The weasel and the whale
And the fin and the tail
The bison and the bird
And even the absurd
- Perhaps that's us
For your Creation, Father, we praise you.

Amen

We thank you, O Lord, for all the beauty of
Nature. Everything is so wonderfully made, we
can only marvel at Your handiwork. Teach us
to discover more and more about the wonders of
Your creation and how to look after it and
keep it beautiful as You meant it to be.

Amen

The last chapter was concerned with thanking
God for all he has given us, and does for us.
This chapter recognises that there are many
problems and difficulties that face us in this
life, and that we should pray for help to cope
with them. The children should be encouraged
to feel that they never have to cope alone,
and that God will never allow them to be faced
with a problem that is beyond their inner
strength to bear.

STARTING OUT

O God our loving Master, show us, we pray You, Your plan for our lives. You know all our weaknesses, our talents and our place in Your creation. Teach us to make the most of our opportunities to serve others and to work steadily towards the goal which You will, in due time reveal to us. May we seek humbly to please You in all our doings. To listen to your voice when facing important decisions, and above all, to be content in the knowledge of Your loving care in all the trials and adversities of life. Day by day, keep us in touch with Your Holy Spirit, through Jesus Christ our Lord.

Amen

SUCCESS

We come to you with grateful hearts, O Lord. You helped us to keep calm and steady and to do our best.
Stay with us now as we go on to the next test. We shall always trust in your help and guidance.

Amen

CRISIS

Against my fear Jesus, stir faith
In place of trembling Father, arouse courage
Into this solitude Holy Spirit, pour comfort

Amen

SUFFERING

Father our hearts are open to you as we would
cry.
In Christ your children's suffering you did
not deny.

Let our souls accept your will for us now
In faith and trust as your Son showed how

Where worldly temptations would carve us
hollow
We look to your Life and Kingdom to follow

Amen

We need Your help, O Lord, to understand the
reason for all the suffering in this world.
Why, for instance children and old people are
so often the victims of wars. Why the lives
of useful, good and caring people are cut
short by some incurable disease.

We know that man himself is responsible for
much of the suffering caused by selfishness
and sin. May we always be on our guard to
make sure that others do not come to harm
through our own negligence and self-will.

Help us to realise that we must all be
prepared to share in the world's suffering in
some way. It is often through the courage of
those that suffer that we learn something of
Your Love in Christ Jesus.

Amen

LEAVING SCHOOL

Soon, Lord, we shall have left school. The whole set-up of our lives will be different; new and unfamiliar. New places and faces, new ways of working and new bosses to please. Go with us, Lord into this daunting world. Give us Your strength and confidence. Whatever we are asked to do may we cheerfully do our best. For the sake of Him Whose Spirit will ever be our guide and Friend.

Amen

SERVICE

O God, our Father, who sent your son, Jesus Christ, into the world - not to be ministered unto, but to minister; teach us likewise, to serve you with gladness. Help us to be on the lookout for opportunities of service in your name, wherever they may lead us. May we look to Christ as our Example, and to His teaching as our guide.

Amen

A PLEA FOR THE HOLY SPIRIT

O God our Father in Heaven, may we always feel Your presence near us. We have Your promise that the Holy Spirit will help and strengthen us, as we fight against the many temptations that will come our way. We do not ask to be spared the trials and difficulties of life, but only to be given peace of mind and heart in the knowledge that, with Your help, we are following the example set by Jesus Christ our Lord.

Amen

CONSCIENCE

O God, our Heavenly Father, teach us to listen to the voice of Conscience. There are so many voices claiming our attention today that we sometimes forget Your still, small voice within us. Help us to cling to what we know to be right, against all temptation. Give us the courage to stand up for our faith in God when put to the test. For the sake of Your Son, Christ Jesus our Lord.

Amen

NATURAL DISASTERS

O Lord our Heavenly Father, we know that your Spirit is with us tonight as we think of the people of.......... who have suffered....... May help reach them quickly. Stir the hearts of all people who are able to help with money or clothing or medicine to respond quickly to appeals. We, in this country, are so thankful that such disasters are so rare here. Help us to show our gratitude by our generous response of help in any way.

Once again, Lord, accept our praise and thanks for all the blessings of this life. For good health, family and friends. Above all for your example for us to follow.

Amen

AFTER AN ACCIDENT

Loving Father, we bring before You tonight our friend and fellow Member....... who is in hospital. Forgive us, Lord, if the accident was in any way caused by our carelessness or disregard of the rules. Help us to be especially careful when younger children are taking part in games with us.

Stay with........in hospital, and help him to bear any pain with courage. May we always obey rules which have been made for our safety. It is not clever to risk injury to ourselves or others. We ask You to lay your healing hand on.......and restore him to full health again, for Jesus Christ's sake.

Amen

BOASTING

Lord, keep me from all boastful thoughts. I like to hear the praise of teachers and friends, but I must remember that all abilities - all skills of hand and eye come from You, who gave us life itself. May I always 'play down' any success of mine, and be ready to encourage and help those who find things difficult, try as they may. For Jesus sake.

Amen

THE HOMELESS

Loving Father, our thoughts today are with the homeless of our town and country. We have the good fortune to be living in comfort and security. Do not let us forget the many hundreds in our cities who have no home or family to go to. May we support, in Your Name, every effort that is being made, locally and nationally to provide shelter and friendship to these lonely people. For the sake of Jesus Christ, who had nowhere to go to lay His head.

Amen

ILLNESS AND DISABILITY

We ask You, Loving Father to lay Your healing
hand on......... She is being very brave, and
we want her to feel You are near her all the
time and bringing her comfort. Help her to
get better, Lord. We all miss her.

Amen

Thank You, God, for the precious gift of
sight. Help us to take every opportunity to
help the sightless. Not only in practical
ways, but in spending time to talk about the
unseen world around them and sharing our
pleasure in the beauties of nature.

Amen

Thank You, God, for the precious gift of
hearing. Give us patience when we try to
communicate with those who live in a silent
world. Show us ways of relieving their
loneliness. They need friendship more than
most.

Amen

We thank You, loving Father
For eyes and ears and taste
Our health and strength are to enjoy
To use - and not to waste

Help us to keep our bodies free
From laziness and sloth -
From yielding to the Tempter's way
Of envy, greed - or both

Holy Spirit, faithful Friend
We know your loving heart
Keep us forever at your side
Nor to the wrong depart

Amen

Loving Father, we bring to You....... who is
undergoing surgery. Give him the strength and
courage to face whatever lies ahead, in the
knowledge that You will always be beside him
in your love and power.

Amen

TEMPTATION

O God, our loving Father, we thank You for all the benefits we enjoy as members of our great Movement. May we never forget what we owe to the founder and his helpers. To all the leaders who have followed his example and teaching. Keep us faithful to our promises and commitments as members.

Help us O Lord to be obedient to the voice of conscience. You know how hard it is to withstand temptation. To go with the crowd into some activity we know to be below Your standard. Help us to realise that Your power and love are ever present, giving strength to our weakness and courage to keep fighting temptation in whatever guise it appears. We ask this in the name of our Lord and Saviour, Jesus Christ.

Amen

O God, You know what it is to face temptation. We need Your help today, more than ever to 'withstand all the fiery darts of the devil'. We are encouraged to take part in, or read about, activities which we know to be wrong and against Your will for us. It is hard to resist and stand alone.

Keep us steadfast, Lord, in clinging to what we know to be right. Give us peace in the knowledge that You understand, and will give us power to overcome, through Jesus Christ your son.

Amen

FORGIVENESS

Lord of the Universe, sun and stars
Creator of Venus, Mercury, Mars
How can such a God as You
Notice what a child can do?

I'm sure You do, however strange
I know Your love can never change
Rejoicing with us when we win -
And suffering with us when we sin

Loving Father, high in Heaven
Thank You for the grace that's given
To us mortals here below
Your pardon, and Your love to know

Amen

As children grow older, they develop more
sophisticated feelings about the world about
them, and their place in it. This chapter
explores some of those feelings and offers
prayers that address them. Once again, the
children would probably find it quite easy to
write prayers about things that they feel
deeply about. They may, however, be less
willing to share these with others, and their
privacy should be respected.

FOR COMPANIONSHIP

When I go tramping over hills
That look towards the starlit sea
Under a sky of windy clouds
Christ of Emmaus, walk with me

Amen

FOR GOOD HUMOUR

"Give me a healthy body, Lord
Give me the sense to keep it so
Also a heart that is not bored
Whatever work I have to do

Give me a sense of humour, Lord
Give me the power to see a joke
To get some happiness from Life
And pass it on to other folk"

Amen   Thomas Henry Basil Webb

DOUBT

I come to You, Lord, with many doubts. I've
had a disappointing day. You seem far-off and
unreal. Make this time pass quickly. I need
to feel Your Presence near me. I know I shall
feel differently tomorrow - once again Your
love will reach me. Your Spirit will be
renewed in my heart and encouraged once more I
will be strong.

Amen

FEAR

Help me to overcome fear, Lord. Fear of the unknown, fear of the future, fear of failure in life. Sometimes I feel so weak against the temptations all around. Let me feel Thy strength upholding me. Thy love enfolding me, and Thy Spirit giving me confidence and banishing all fear.

Amen

WHEN WE ARE SORRY

Lord Jesus, I'm sorry I lost my temper today. Help me to stay silent when I'm angry, to make up a quarrel, rather than to start it. May I seek Your peace, now and always.

Amen

Loving Father, I'm sorry for what happened today. You know what I mean. You know everything. All the same, I know that you still love me. Please help me to put this behind me and try not to let it happen again. With Your help I'll try hard.

Amen

"Forgive me, Lord, for Thy dear Son
The ill that I this day have done
That with the world, myself and Thee
I, ere I sleep, at peace may be".

Amen   (Bishop Thomas Ken 1637-1711)

41

How many times this day I've missed
The chance to do some good
And left unsaid some cheering word
Because of my 'bad mood'

I'm sorry, Lord. Forgive me.

Amen

WHEN WE ARE SAD

Loving Father, You know why we are sad today.
Help us to bear the unhappy times, knowing
that You understand how we feel. Your loving
Spirit is always beside us. Help us to cheer
up and live happily again.

Amen

Moods and emotions arrive and leave Lord
You know that this sadness has arrived in my
heart
I pray that Your joy and peace break through
Lord
And leave me securely in your caring presence.

Amen

Everything seems to be wrong, I am wrong
Nothing succeeds and no one cares
Please change my life for me
As I seek, Father, let me find.

Amen

WHEN WE ARE HAPPY

Life shined for me today Jesus
Let me shine for you

Amen

It's good to be alive
To run, to ride, to swim
To You, our Heavenly Father
We raise a thankful hymn

Amen

Today has been great, Lord Jesus
You heard how we laughed and played!
You certainly shared our high spirits
We felt You were near - and You stayed!

Amen

A happy day, a gift indeed
In our hearts a joy took seed
Lord in our joy we ask of you
To share your blessing with others too.

Amen

43

Many young people experience their first night away from home and parents when at camp. These prayers are based upon the concerns and pleasures they will have whilst in the strange new world of camp.

Thank You, Lord for another good day, here
at.........
Thank You for eyes to see the beauty of the
countryside.
Thank You for ears to hear the song of the
birds and the wind in the trees.
Thank You for strong limbs and good health.
Thank You for the fresh, clean air which
surrounds us.
Be with us through the night. Bless our
families at home and let them know that we are
thinking of them with love.

Amen

Thank You God for giving me
A healthy appetite
Not only for the food I eat
But all things good and right
For happy songs and camp fire fun
For swimming in the sea
For seeking after loyal friends -
You have been good to me!

Amen

O, God our Father, we are gathered here in
this beautiful part of your creation. We
thank You for all the joys of the countryside.
For the fresh, clean air and the chance of a
break from our routine life. Help us to make
the most of our time here. To get to know
each other better, to share the daily chores
fairly, to explore the wonders of Nature, and,
above all, to rejoice in the knowledge of Thy
great love for the children of men. In the
name of Jesus Christ our Lord.

Amen

THIS PAGE IS LEFT BLANK FOR YOU TO ADD YOUR
OWN PRAYERS

THIS PAGE IS LEFT BLANK FOR YOU TO ADD YOUR OWN PRAYERS

THIS PAGE IS LEFT BLANK FOR YOU TO ADD YOUR
OWN PRAYERS